THE BIBLE AND THE CROSS

THE BIBLE AND
THE CROSS

G. CAMPBELL MORGAN

WIPF & STOCK · Eugene, Oregon

Wipf and Stock Publishers
199 W 8th Ave, Suite 3
Eugene, OR 97401

The Bible and the Cross
By Morgan, G. Campbell
Copyright©1909 by Morgan, G. Campbell
ISBN 13: 978-1-5326-1767-6
Publication date 2/2/2017
Previously published by
Fleming H. Revell, Co., 1909

G. CAMPBELL MORGAN REPRINT SERIES

FOREWORD

If it is true that the measure of a person's greatness is their influence, not only on his own time but also on future generations, G. Campbell Morgan must be regarded as a great person. His greatness is seen not only in the wide impact of his ministry on both sides of the Atlantic, but in the fact that his books are still read and studied sixty five years after his death. Named one of the ten greatest preachers of the twentieth-century by the contributing board of Preaching magazine, Morgan made the Bible a new and living book not only to the congregations who listened to him, but the vast multitude of persons who read his books.

Fox sixty-seven years Morgan preached and taught the Scriptures and served churches in England and the United States. What is remarkable is that his commentaries and expositions of the Bible still speak to persons of a new millennium. There have been many changes in the world since he faithfully preached and taught the Scriptures, but the wide appeal of his books testify to the timelessness of his message.

Although he held pastorates in the Congregational and Presbyterian denominations, he had an ecumenical appeal to persons of all denominations and traditions. The mystic Thomas á Kempis once wrote, "He to whom the eternal word speaks is delivered from many opinions." In one of his sermons, he referred to the words of Amos that there would be a famine for hearing the word of God (Amos 8:11). The timeless work of G. Campbell Morgan addresses that hunger, as his books enable his readers to get beyond opinions to the living Word.

Wipf and Stock Publishers have rendered a great gift to the religious world in reprinting dozens of Morgan's books. This growing collection makes his books more available, so that readers have an option other than searching the internet for used, and often expensive, copies. Among this collection is the classic *The Great Physician* and commentaries on the Gospel of Matthew and John. Persons seeking a living faith and a meaningful encounter with God would profit from reading any of these Morgan books.

Near the end of his ministry, in a sermon entitled "But One Thing," Morgan commented on how Portugal changed the words of a coin after Christopher Columbus discovered America. No longer did the inscription say, *Ne Plus Ultra* (nothing more beyond) but *Plus Ultra* (more beyond). It is the hope of the G. Campbell Morgan Trust that the reprinting of these books will bring readers to the "more beyond," and an even deeper encounter with the Word in Scripture.

The Morgan Trust
Richard L. Morgan
Howard C. Morgan
John C. Morgan

CONTENTS

I
THE DEATH OF JESUS: UNNATURAL 9

II
THE DEATH OF CHRIST: SUPERNATURAL .. 27

III
THE DEATH OF THE LORD: RECONCILING .. 45

IV
THE CROSS AND THE SINNER 65

V
THE CROSS AND THE SAINT 87

VI
THE CROSS AND THE AGES TO COME 109

THE DEATH OF JESUS: UNNATURAL

I

THE DEATH OF JESUS: UNNATURAL

"Ye men of Israel, hear these words: Jesus of Nazareth, a Man approved of God unto you by mighty works and wonders and signs, which God did by Him in the midst of you, as ye yourselves know; Him, being delivered up by the determinate counsel and foreknowledge of God, ye by the hand of lawless men did crucify and slay."—ACTS ii. 22,23.

"Ye denied the Holy and Righteous One, and asked for a murderer to be granted unto you, and killed the Prince of Life."—ACTS iii. 14, 15.

THE present series of studies assumes that the Christian religion is the religion of the Lord Jesus Christ, and that the Bible is its authoritative exposition.

Of the Christian system, the Cross of Christ is the central truth. It is at once a profound mystery, and a most glorious revelation. As to its deepest and hidden method it is a mystery; in its unveiling of the heart of God, and in the declaration of the possibility of the forgiveness of sins, it is a revelation.

Our purpose is to gather about the Cross in order that we may consider it in the light of Bible teaching. I shall endeavour resolutely to avoid making any appeal to speculations or philosophies which are not founded on acceptance of the authority of Scripture.

The two passages which indicate our starting-point contain much teaching with which I do not propose now to deal. I refer to them because they set forth certain truths of supreme importance to our argument. The quotations are taken respectively from the first and second discourses of Peter, delivered in the power of the outpoured Spirit. It has often been pointed out that a comparison of the Apostles before and after Pentecost reveals a most remarkable change in them, resulting from the coming of the Spirit. In nothing was this change more marked than in their attitude to the Cross. In the last days of our Lord's ministry, during which He foretold His Cross with great distinctness, these men quite honestly believed that the Cross would inevitably mean the defeat of His purpose, and disaster to His enterprise. Immediately after the reception of the Spirit they referred to the Cross in such language as to make it plain that there had come to them an entirely new conception of its meaning.

In each of these passages Peter emphasized two facts: first, that of the sinlessness of Jesus; and secondly, that of the sin of His murder. The sinlessness of Jesus is declared in the first in the words, "Jesus of Nazareth, a Man approved of God unto you by mighty works and wonders and signs, which God did by Him in the midst of you, as ye yourselves know." The meaning of the Apostle is perfectly plain. He affirmed that the Man Jesus was proven by His miracles and wonders and signs to be a perfect Man.

When, in the second passage, the Apostle charged those to whom he spoke with having slain "the Holy and Righteous One," his words were carefully chosen. The word "holy" describes inward purity, which is the perfection of character. The word "righteous" describes active rectitude, which is perfection of conduct. Thus Peter affirmed that Jesus Whom they slew was both "holy," that is, pure in character; and "righteous," that is, true in conduct.

He moreover, in each case charged upon the men to whom he was speaking that their putting to death of a sinless Man was an act of sin. We are thus confronted with a problem which we are compelled to recognize, and of which we must attempt to find the solution. That solution is not found in these passages, and we shall not reach it in this study. The matter of first importance is that we should recognize the problem.

Let me state that problem briefly. In the midst of that universe which the Bible declares to be under the government of God, the one perfect Man in all human history is put to death by the hands of sinful men. Men of impure character slay the one Man of purity of character. Men of unrighteous conduct put to death the one Man of righteous conduct. The fact thus barely stated suggests the problem.

Let us attempt to see this more clearly.

UNNATURAL 13

This we shall do if we consider the teaching of the Bible concerning death and Jesus; for such consideration must inevitably reveal the fact that the death of Jesus was unnatural—that is, something out of the regular order, something that demands explanation beyond that which accounts for the death of other human beings.

I

What does the Bible teach concerning death? In answer to that inquiry I shall first state the case in general propositions, and then make one or two references to particular passages of Scripture. The Bible teaches that death in the case of man is the direct outcome of sin, and the penalty thereof. It declares, moreover, that death essentially consists in the separation of the spirit of man from the Spirit of Life, which is the Spirit of God. It further teaches that this separation of the spirit of man from the Spirit of God involves ultimately, if not immediately, the separation of man's spirit from man's body. It finally teaches that the separation between the spirit of man and the Spirit of God may be an age-abiding separation. In this connection it must carefully be borne in mind that this teaching refers to human nature, which is more than animal nature. Between the two there is a great gulf fixed. Whatever the process of human creation may have been, the Scripture clearly teaches that man became a "living soul" by the direct act of God, and that there is an impassable gulf between man and every other form of life. This moreover, is acknowledged true as the result of investigation, as well as in the light of Scripture teaching. I do not think it necessary for me to argue that at length, yet it is necessary to state it if we are to understand the meaning of death in the case of man. Man is the offspring of God, made in His image, and in His likeness. That declaration has no reference to anything that is merely physical or animal in man's life. Human personality to-day has a physical basis, an animal tenement in which man dwells; but, according to the uniform teaching of Scripture, man is essentially spirit, as God is

Spirit. Death, therefore, fundamentally and finally is the separation of the spirit of man from the Spirit of God. It is, moreover, a penalty, and a penalty ceases to be a penalty if the person upon whom it is imposed cease to exist. The death penalty is essentially that of the separation of man, as a spirit, from God Who is Spirit. The issue of this separation is separation between the spirit of the man and his body, though that may not immediately follow the fundamental separation. Death as separation may become age-abiding.

According to the Genesis story, the warning given to the first man was, "In the day that thou eatest thereof thou shalt surely die"; and in the day of their disobedience our first parents died, in that they were separated by that act from God. After they had sinned God said, "Dust thou art, and unto dust shalt thou return." This word was not uttered until sin had been committed. That was the sentence of death. The spirit of man in the moment of its rebellion lost its connection with the Spirit of God, and the separation between his spirit and his body commenced.

In the Epistle to the Romans, in one of the briefest phrases, Paul declared that "through one man sin entered into the world, and *death through sin.*" I am not proposing to argue these subjects in the light of any human philosophy, or even of scientific knowledge, and yet in passing I am constrained to say that no man of science has even been able to explain the reason why all men die. The teaching of Scripture is that death is the outcome of sin. Had there been no sin there would have been no death. This, of course, applies only to the human race. In the animal world, and indeed, through all the lower forms of life, death was the end of being; but when it invaded the human race it came as the direct result of sin and as its penalty. In the obedient life there is no place for death. As in the case of Christ, life passes from the probationary to the larger and fuller experience by transfiguration or metamorphosis. Man sinning is immediately dead in the deepest meaning of the word, in that he is alienated from God. The issue of that is separation from his body, and finally his age-abiding separation from God. To summarize the rapid survey: death is the wage of sin, its issue, its result, its penalty. All that pall which rests upon humanity today by reason of death is demonstration of the government of God. Whether the sinner be rich or poor, high or low, bond or free, he cannot escape the penalty of his sin.

II

In the light of this consideration we now turn to our second inquiry as to the teaching of Scripture concerning Jesus. I am careful for the moment not to speak of Him as Christ or Lord, but only by the name by which He was known in Nazareth, by which His disciples and His familiar friends knew Him—the name which marks Him out as a Man among men. Concerning Him as the Scripture teaches that He was absolutely sinless, and that in that respect He was an exception in human history. He made this claim for Himself in many ways; but two illustrations will suffice. In an atmosphere surcharged with criticism He declared, "I do always the things that are pleasing to Him." It is impossible to imagine these words having been spoken by any other. The great teachers of the world, saints of bygone ages, and the saints of to-day have all confessed their own failure. Jesus made no such confession, but rather declared that He always pleased God. The other quotation occurs in the same surroundings. He challenged the men who were criticising His claims, as He asked them, "Which of you convinceth Me of sin?" and to this challenge their only answer was silence.

Turning from His own testimony to that of others recorded in the New Testament, we find that at His baptism, God said, "This is My beloved Son, in Whom I am well pleased." On the Mount of Transfiguration, to the astonished disciples the Voice out of heaven made the same declaration. And again, when Jesus approaching the hour of His passion, prayed, "Father, glorify Thy name," the answering Voice declared, "I have both glorified it, and will glorify it again." Thus the testimony of God, Who is the sworn foe of all evil, the One Who can by no means clear the guilty, affirmed the sinlessness of Jesus.

The testimony of His own disciples was equally clear. Peter called him "the Holy and Righteous One"; John wrote of Him, "In Him is no sin"; and Paul declared of Him that He "knew no sin."

Impartial witnesses—that is, those not to be found among the number of His disciples—gave utterance to the same truth. The one voice raised on His behalf in the hour of His sorest need—that of Pilate's wife—referred to Him as "that righteous Man." The malefactor, dying by His side on the Cross, declared, "This Man hath done nothing amiss." The Roman centurion, observing Him in the awful hour of death, said, "Certainly this was a righteous Man."

The testimony of evil men is the same. The time-serving and scheming Pilate, who fain would have saved both his conscience and his position, thrice declared, "I find no crime in Him." That was the language of a judge. Charges had been brought against Jesus. Pilate investigated them, and this was his verdict. Judas, in the terrible hour when the consciousness of the guilt of his treachery broke upon his soul, hurried into the presence of the chief priests, and, flinging down the ill-gotten silver, cried in remorse, "I have sinned in that I have betrayed innocent blood."

Or finally, take the testimony of an evil spirit who declared to Jesus, "I know Thee Who Thou art, the Holy One of God."

Thus upon His own testimony, upon the testimony of God, upon the testimony of His disciples, upon the testimony of impartial witnesses, upon the testimony of evil men, upon the testimony of a demon, we declare that Jesus of Nazareth was sinless.

To the accuracy of that testimony the centuries bear witness. Men who deny all we believe concerning the deeper mystery of the Person of Jesus yet admit the sinlessness of His human life. Through nineteen centuries no reputable critic of Jesus has ever questioned this claim.

All this finally leads to the conclusion that the death of Jesus was unnatural—that is to say, it was out of the true order of human life according to the economy of God. Death is the outcome of sin. Jesus was sinless. Nevertheless He died. I have taken so long to state the problem because it is only as we are arrested by the uniqueness of this death, by the strangeness of it, by the baffling perplexity of its problem, that we are ever likely to discover its true meaning.

These then, are the problems which arise. If Jesus were only man as I am man, then according to the teaching of the Bible concerning death and concerning Himself, His death violated the moral order of the universe. We speak to-day of the problem of pain, of the problem of evil, as these are revealed in the conditions and circumstances of human life the world over. I admit them all; but without hesitation declare that no event in human history, no circumstance of human suffering, has ever been chronicled which is so overwhelmingly perplexing as this death of Jesus. If He were man merely as I am, sharer of my nature, and nothing more, and were perfectly sinless, then His death constitutes the severest reflection on the righteousness of the government of God that the world has ever seen. Here is a problem that demands examination. There must be some meaning in this death beyond anything that appears as the result of surface observation. To find the explanation I must turn to other passages of Scripture than those with which we commenced the present study.

Suffering and death resulting from sin demonstrate the righteous government of God. I know there are mysteries on the plane of our every-day life. Until this hour we see the righteous suffering for the guilty in some lower sense. And yet all that we call righteous are also sinners, and in their suffering do but enter into the fellowship of that which results from the sin in which they also share. Here however, is a case of an absolutely sinless One—a case of One Who, to use that marvellous phrase of the New Testament which we too little understand, was "separate from sinners,"—handed over, as Peter distinctly declares, "by the determinate counsel and foreknowledge of God" to a violent death at the hands of lawless men.

Our proposition then is, that the suffering and death of Jesus demand some explanation. If He be indeed only man, and if He be sinless as He claimed to be, as God declared Him to be, as men witnessed Him to be, as devils owned Him to be, and yet died; then His death is the crime of all crimes, and in it the moral order was violated as nowhere else.

We pause here. The death of Jesus is unnatural. We ask for an explanation. We shall only find it as we turn to a fuller revelation of Scripture concerning Him and His death than the scope of this study has permitted. At the moment we have arrived at this point; death is the wage of sin; Jesus was sinless, and therefore, He ought not to have died. Why did He die?

THE DEATH OF CHRIST:
SUPERNATURAL

II

THE DEATH OF CHRIST: SUPERNATURAL

"I lay down my life, that I may take it again. No one taketh it away from Me, but I lay it down of Myself. I have power to lay it down, and I have power to take it again. This commandment received I from My Father."—JOHN x. 17, 18.

IT is not at all surprising to read what immediately follows this declaration, "There arose a division again among the Jews because of these words. And many of them said, He hath a devil, and is mad; why hear ye Him? Others said, These are not the sayings of one possessed with a devil. Can a devil open the eyes of the blind?"

I sometimes think that no words of our Lord which have been recorded for us have received less serious attention than these, and yet they constitute the very heart of all His teaching concerning Himself and His mission.

28   THE DEATH OF CHRIST:

I do not propose to consider this passage alone or exhaustively. I have read it because it seems to me the most remarkable statement Jesus ever made concerning His death; and because, in association with other words of His, it will enable us to follow a little further the teaching of the Bible concerning the Cross.

The problem of the death of Jesus considered in our previous study is solved when we contemplate it from the standpoint of what the Scriptures teach concerning the meaning of His title—the Christ. The death of Christ was supernatural because Christ was supernatural.

I am very conscious of the awkwardness of that word supernatural. All the things of which we speak as supernatural are only supernatural to our finite knowledge and understanding. The things of which we speak as miraculous are only so because we know certain laws, but are not acquainted with the whole economy of God. In the ages to come, and in the light of the Father's house, we shall not speak of these things as supernatural, we shall discover that they are all in harmony with the nature of God. For the sake of accommodating our meditation on this subject to the necessities of our present limitation we are however compelled to speak of the death of Christ as supernatural. If we speak of Jesus as the Man of Nazareth only, sinless, spotless, undefiled, then we affirm that His death was unnatural, that is, out of the regular order. When we see Him as Christ, we are driven to the conclusion that His death was supernatural.

Let us then consider the teaching of our Lord concerning Himself, and concerning His death, in order to make certain deductions concerning the death of Christ from that teaching.

I

First, then, the teaching of Christ concerning Himself. The word Christ is, of course, the Greek form of the Hebrew word Messiah. Passing in review the occasions upon which our Lord made use of the word, we shall see what was His conception of its meaning, and what He intended men to understand thereby.

I find in the course of the four gospels

that He is quoted as referring to the title directly or indirectly as applied to Himself ten times.

His first claim to be the Christ was made where of all places one would least expect to find it; not to the Hebrew people, but in Samaria; not to Samaria as represented in a large assembly, but to Samaria as represented in a woman; and, most astonishing of all, to Samaria as represented in a woman of sin and shame. He had uttered in her hearing that wonderful declaration that "the hour cometh, when neither in this mountain, nor in Jerusalem, shall ye worship the Father....the hour cometh, and now is, when the true worshippers shall worship the Father in spirit and in truth: for such doth the Father seek to be His worshippers"; and she having replied, "I know that Messiah cometh; when He is come, He will declare unto us all things," He said, "I that speak unto thee am He."

The next occasion of definite reference to the title was at Cæsarea Philippi, when He questioned the disciples as to what men said about Him. Peter having answered,

"Thou art the Christ, the Son of the living God," He commanded them that they were to tell no man that He was the Christ.

His next reference to the fact that He was the Christ was incidental. John had told Him that they had forbidden one whom they had seen casting out devils in the name of Jesus, because he followed not with them. Jesus rebuked him, declaring that those who were not against Him were for Him, and then said this simple but significant thing, revealing His estimate of the dignity of the title Christ; "Whosoever shall give you a cup of water to drink, because ye are Christ's, verily I say unto you, he shall in no wise lose his reward."

A little further on in His ministry, after discoursing on the sheepfold, the flock, and the Good Shepherd, the people were strangely perplexed, and sent a deputation who said, "If thou art the Christ, tell us plainly"; and He replied, "I told you, and ye believe not; the works that I do in My Father's name, these bear witness of Me." Thus He claimed to be the Christ, and declared that the truth of His claim was demonstrated by His works.

Next in order is the occasion when He challenged the rulers concerning the meaning of Messiahship, "What think ye of the Christ?" The question did not mean, What do you think of Me? He asked them what their religious conception was of the Messiah for whom they were looking. "Whose son is He?" They said, "The Son of David." He did not contradict them, but asked another question, "How then doth David in the Spirit call him Lord?" The problem as He presented it to them revealed His own conception of the meaning of the title; Christ is Son of David, of his very nature; yet Lord of David, and thus in some way superior to him.

Almost immediately after this conflict with the rulers, He said to His disciples, "One is your Master, even the Christ." You will need guidance and direction; the Christ will be your one Master, one Guide, one Director.

A little later He warned them, saying, "There shall arise false Christs." "If any man shall say unto you, Lo, here is the Christ, or, Here; believe it not." "For many shall come in My name, saying, I am the Christ: and shall lead many astray."

A little later He again spoke of Himself as the Christ, "This is life eternal, that they should know Thee the only true God, and Him Whom Thou didst send, even Jesus Christ."

At the end the high priest challenged Him, "I adjure Thee by the living God, that Thou tell us whether Thou be the Christ, the Son of God." The three Evangelists give different answers, and there is every reason to believe that the whole of them were given. Matthew gives His reply as, "Thou hast said"; Mark as simply, "I am"; Luke tells us that He parried them with a statement which was a rebuke, "If I tell you, ye will not believe: and if I ask you, ye will not answer."

Finally, on the other side of the Cross He made use of the same title, thus: "Behoved it not the Christ to suffer these things and to enter into His glory?.... It is written, that the Christ should suffer and rise again from the dead the third day, and that repentance and remission of sins should be preached."

From the teaching of all these references I make these deductions.

According to Christ's own estimate of the meaning of the title, Christ is first Son of Man, David's Son; but He is also Son of God, David's Lord. The title fits a Person Who is of human nature, but Who is infinitely more than of human nature.

The mission of Christ—I am not now speaking of its process or its method, but of its ultimate intention—according to His own conception, was to give the knowledge which leads to worship, to give that knowledge which in itself is age-abiding life. "This is life eternal, that they should know Thee the only true God, and Him Whom Thou didst send, even Jesus Christ." The mission of the Christ was that of bringing men to such knowledge of God as should constrain them to the attitude of worship, and give them age-abiding life.

His teaching moreover, reveals His conception of the process by which the Christ would accomplish that work to be that of suffering, dying, rising from the dead, and giving men repentance and remission of sins.

II

Secondly, the teaching of Christ concerning His own death. I shall now still further restrict our outlook to the Gospel of John. Repeated reference is made therein to an hour toward which Christ was evidently looking. At Cana of Galilee, when His mother suggested that He should work a miracle, He said, "Mine hour is not yet come." When a little later we find Him in the temple, and opposition and hatred were stirred up against Him, and men would fain have laid hold on Him, it is declared that they could not do so, "because His hour was not yet come." Still later, while He was teaching in the treasury, men desired to arrest Him, and again the declaration is made, "His hour was not yet come." When the Greeks were asking to see Him, He said, "The hour is come that the Son of Man should be glorified." The reference was evidently to the Cross, for immediately He said, "Except a grain of wheat fall into the earth and die, it abideth by itself alone." The Paschal discourses are introduced by the statement that Jesus, "knowing that His hour was come...... having loved His own which were in the world, He loved them unto the end"; and later, in the course of them, He distinctly declared to His disciples, "The hour cometh, yea, is come, that ye shall be scattered, every man to his own, and shall leave Me alone: and yet I am not alone, because the Father is with Me." Finally, in the great intercessory prayer, He said, "Father, the hour is come."

That is a rapid survey, but it helps us to see that from the very beginning Christ knew that the culminating fact in His ministry was death.

Then examine the facts of His death as recorded by John. Jesus, despised and rejected of men, passed down into the sombre shade of Gethsemane's olive-garden, and spent a night of anguish. Suddenly, towards daybreak, there was seen the lurid glare of torches; and Judas came with armed men and a mob. Jesus confronted them, with that poor little handful of men standing behind Him. He asked them naturally, "Whom seek ye?" The answer was quick and ready, "Jesus of Nazareth." He said, "I am," and they fell backward to the ground. There is no possibility of escape from the conviction that there was something—whether in the tone of the voice or in the flash of the eye, I know not—by which these men were made conscious of power which they feared; and for the moment they dared lay no arresting hand upon Him. There followed an almost greater marvel. These men recovered themselves, persuaded themselves in all likelihood, as men can so easily do, that the vision was nought, that the flaming glory was only a phantasm. Herein is the wonder that He Who could so say, "I am," as to compel men to prostration and to overpowering weakness, permitted Himself to be bound. This was a demonstration of the truth of His assertion, "No man taketh My life from Me, I lay it down of Myself." This was Jesus of Nazareth, but He was more. This is a mystery, a marvel, but yet it is the solution of the first problem. So much was He Jesus of Nazareth that they could seize Him and bind Him; so much more was He than Jesus of Nazareth that, when He but said, "I am," they became as dead men in His presence.

I follow Him along the sorrowful way to Pilate's judgment-bar, and watch the perplexity of Pilate. Some day, when you are in doubt about Jesus, about His Deity, about His imperial, lonely, splendid dignity, read that story again. I now touch it at one point only. Pilate, perplexed, astonished, and harassed, at last looked into the face of this Man in the loneliness of the inner chamber to which he had taken Him, and said in effect: You know I have power over you; You are in my hands. Jesus looked back into the face of Pilate and said, "Thou wouldest have no power against Me, except it were given thee from above." From that time Pilate worked hard to set Him free, but he was unable to do it. The explanation is to be found in His declaration, "I lay down My life ....no one taketh it from Me."

SUPERNATURAL 39

Once again, I pass beyond that scene in Pilate's hall to the Cross itself. Here I can only speak in halting words. The longer I live, the less I can say in the actual presence of that Cross. Yet God help us to see this. In all the mystery of the wounding and the darkness never lose sight of the regal dignity of His dying. When He knew that all things were accomplished He said "I thirst." That is Jesus of Nazareth. Then He said, "It is finished; and He bowed His head, and gave up His Spirit." That is the Christ, dying by His own will and act.

In the light of these considerations it is evident that He clearly apprehended His death, but He definitely accepted it as the issue of His ministry. There were moments when His soul was troubled, when He said, "Now is My soul troubled"; but He also said, "Father, glorify Thy name." Thus He triumphed.

Finally, the death of Jesus was *accomplished*. That is the word used in one of the synoptic gospels. Moses and Elijah talked, not of the death He should die, but of the exodus He should "accomplish."

In our last study we saw the hands of lawless men murder Jesus, and so far as they were concerned it was murder brutal and wicked; and, if I want to know what sin is, I do not consult any new philosophy, but that Cross. In this study we see the deeper matter. Peter said, "Jesus of Nazareth....ye by the hand of lawless men did crucify and slay"; but Peter also said, "Him, being delivered up by the determinate counsel and foreknowledge of God." This Christ, Who is God's Son as well as David's Son, David's Lord as well as David's Heir, this One went to the Cross, died at His own time and by His own choice, apprehending the death, accepting the death, accomplishing the death.

From this study we may make these deductions. Christ was supernatural, and therefore His death must be considered in the light of that fact. Jesus of Nazareth was Man of my manhood, but He was more. When we speak of His death we must not speak of it merely as the death of a man. We must take into account His supernatural nature when we would understand His death. Therefore the death of

Christ was unique. There are some wonderful stories of dying, heroic dying, dastardly dying, noble dying, ignoble dying; but this story is unmatched in literature.

If this be only a dream, a fancy, then I am constrained to say, as I am always constrained to say in the presence of these stories, in God's name, find me the man who dreamed it. My affirmation is that no man could have dreamed this. It is unique, lonely. It is the story of the death of One Who was at once Son of God and Son of Man.

It was a death in which the consciousness of God and the consciousness of man were identified. God's consciousness of man found expression when the dying One said, "My God, My God, why hast Thou forsaken Me?" That was the cry of God as He gathered into His own heart all the consciousness of humanity in its lack of Him.

Man's consciousness of God found expression as the One upon the Cross said, "It is finished," and "Father, into Thy hands I commend My Spirit."

If you would write the truth of the

Cross in the briefest words you must borrow the language of the Apostle and write it thus, "God was in Christ, reconciling the world unto Himself."

The death of Jesus, if He were a Galilean peasant only, was unnatural; but the death of this Christ Who is more than man, was supernatural, and this explains that.

This study teaches us that the subject is beyond us, and that we can only understand the purpose of such dying, as God reveals the meaning to us. It is outside the ken of our philosophy. It is beyond the reach of our speculation. It baffles the wildest flight of our imagination. That God in man should stoop to death creates a new wonder, a new amazement, and I am constrained to ask the reason of such dying.

THE DEATH OF THE LORD:
RECONCILING

III

THE DEATH OF THE LORD: RECONCILING

"You....hath He reconciled in the body of His flesh through death."—COLOSSIANS i. 21, 22.

THE Cross and Resurrection of Jesus completely altered His disciples' conception of Him. It is only necessary to read carefully the Gospel stories, and then immediately, and in contrast, the story contained in the Acts of the Apostles, to see that the attitude of these men toward their Master was entirely changed. I am not suggesting for a single moment that they did not love Him and believe in Him before the Cross; but I do most certainly affirm that they did not understand Him. A new conception of His Lordship came to them as a result of His Resurrection from among the dead. This resulted in a new conception of the Cross. The Cross had appeared to them as supreme tragedy, by which all their hopes were put out, all their expectations disappointed. The Cross became to them the supreme victory, the very way of the life which they had preached. Before the Cross, they had called Him Lord, Master, Teacher; but only in the sense of Teacher, Exemplar, Leader. After the Resurrection the title Lord meant infinitely more than before, for as its light flashed upon the Cross they came to know Christ as they came to know Christ as they had never known Him before. This new conception of the Lordship of Jesus is most clearly set forth in the writings of the Apostles; and nowhere more clearly than in the chapter from which the statement is taken which is the basis of our meditation.

We are now to consider the death of the Lord; and we use the word Lord, not in that earlier, simpler, and incomplete sense in which the disciples used it while Jesus was still with them; but in that larger, fuller, more wonderful sense in which they used it after Pentecost, when they looked back to the Cross through the fact of the Resurrection, in the light of the Spirit.

RECONCILING 47

We have considered the death of Jesus of Nazareth as perfect Man, and declared it was unnatural. We have considered the death of Christ, and declared it to be supernatural, a death which cannot be measured by any other. Now we come to the consideration of the meaning of that death in the economy of God, as revealed to the holy Apostles and writers of the early Church; and we affirm that the death which was unnatural if you measure it by human standards, supernatural if you look upon the Person and glory of Christ, was a reconciling death when He is seen as Lord in the full meaning of the title.

I

Let us first examine the contextual teaching concerning the Lordship of Jesus.

In the earlier part of the chapter we find the Person to Whom the Apostle refers. An actual Person within human comprehension is certainly referred to, as the phrase "the body of His flesh" signifies. In the thirteenth verse these words occur, "Who delivered us out of the power of

48 THE DEATH OF THE LORD:

darkness and translated us into the kingdom of the Son of His love." In the third verse we find these words, "We give thanks to God, the Father of our Lord Jesus Christ."

This then, is the selfsame Person concerning Whom we have been speaking in previous studies as Jesus of Nazareth, and the Christ. He Who was at once David's Son and David's Lord is now spoken of by the Apostle in all the full and gracious dignity of title, name, and office, as "the Lord Jesus Christ." It is of this Person that the Apostle affirms, "You .... hath He reconciled in the body of His flesh through death."

Between these outstanding verses are statements which reveal what the Apostle meant by the Lordship of Christ. In them he declares what the relation of this Person is to God Himself; what the relation of this Person is to the whole creation; and, finally, what the relation of this Person is to the new creation, the Church. His relation to God is expressed in the words, "Who is the Image of the invisible God"; His relation to creation in the words, "In Him were all things created, in the heavens and upon the earth, things visible and things invisible, whether thrones, or dominions, or principalities, or powers; all things have been created through Him, and unto Him, and He is before all things, and in Him all things consist"; His relation to the Church in the words, "He is the Head of the Body, the Church; Who is the Beginning, the Firstborn from the dead; that in all things He might have the pre-eminence."

That is the ultimate teaching of the New Testament concerning the Lordship of Christ. First, He is Lord by the right of His relation to the Father. He is the Image, the Representation, the Unveiling, the Manifestation of the invisible God, Who has no manifestation save through Him. The declaration is not that He became the Image of God; but that He is the Image of God; He is always the Image of God. Or, to use the tenses of human limitation in speaking of the abiding eternities, He was the Image of God long ere time began, ere creation came into being; He will be the Image of God in all the ages

50 THE DEATH OF THE LORD:

yet to come; He is the One through Whom God is always manifest to created beings. Whether they be principalities or powers in the heavenly places; or things of time and sense; whoever they may be, and whenever they may exist, and wherever their habitation may be, God is revealed to them through this Person. That one fact sets Him at once in the place of Lordship over creation; He is indeed, therefore, "KING OF KINGS, AND LORD OF LORDS," absolute and supreme.

But He is Lord also by virtue of His immediate relation to the Creation. All created things exist through the act of this Person. The One Whom men called Jesus was infinitely more than a Man of His own age; He was indeed the Word through Whom creation came into being and He is the One Who upholds all things by the Word of His power; all things consist in Him.

Finally, He is Lord by the mystery of His relation to the Church; He is the Head of the Church. The two expressions which the Apostle uses here concerning this Person in His relation to the first creation,

RECONCILING 51

and to His Church, are full of meaning. When he speaks of the relation of Christ to the first creation he refers to Him as "The Firstborn of all creation." When he speaks of His relation to the Church he describes Him as "The Firstborn from the dead," a far more remarkable thing. "The Firstborn of all creation" suggests that all created things came in the power of His essential life. He commended and it was done. "The Firstborn from the dead" suggests a renewed life, won out of the mystery of death.

In the Roman letter this selfsame Apostle declares, "Concerning His Son, Who was born of the seed of David according to the flesh, Who was declared to be the Son of God with power, according to the Spirit of Holiness, by the resurrection of the dead, even Jesus Christ our Lord." This consciousness of the Lordship of Christ resulted from Resurrection and Pentecost.

This Lord Jesus Christ is the Image of God, the Manifestation of God; He is the originating Creator, and the sustaining might in the universe; He is the One Who came back out of the experience of death, with a new light upon His brow, and new life in His gift. He is the Lord of all, and is declared to be so with power, by the Resurrection from among the dead.

Let us now examine this word *reconciled*. The Greek word signifies, quite literally, an exchange—that is, in this use, a change in relationship, the bringing into fellowship of things which have been opposed. In our text we have a strengthened form of the word, which means to fully change, and therefore suggests complete reconciliation. Both that and the word commonly used suggest change back to an original intention. Reconciliation is return to true position and relationship.

Wherever this word is used in the New Testament in regard to man's relation to God, it indicates a change in man, and not in God. "We were reconciled to God," "God Who hath reconciled us to Himself," "Reconciling the world unto Himself," "Be ye reconciled to God," "That He might reconcile both unto God," "To reconcile all things unto Himself," "You .... now hath He reconciled .... to present you .... before Him.'' While that grouping of Scriptures is incomplete, in that the context in every case is omitted, it does help us to see that the reconciliation of God and the sinner, of which the New Testament treats, is not God's reconciliation to the sinner, but the sinner's reconciliation to God. This is not a distinction without a difference. A clear understanding of it and determined adherence to that method of expression will throw much light upon this death of Christ, through which our reconciliation has been made possible. It is not that through the death of Christ, God may be turned back to the sinner; it is that through the death of Christ the sinner may be turned back to God. This is quite radical and quite important. It does recogize a change in the Divine attitude, from that which man had any right to expect; not an actual change, for God never turned His back upon the sinner. The only occasion in which we find anything approaching God's forsaking man is in the mystery of the Cross. God never turned His face away from man. Sometimes, in moments of anguish, men have been constrained to speak of themselves as God-forsaken. It is never true. Sometimes, in great consciousness of sin, men are constrained to think God has abandoned them. It is not so. God has never, never turned His back upon a sinner.

But now let us carefully remember that He must have done so but for this passion which the mystery of the Cross reveals. Yes, but then there *is* this mystery of the passion, and because of it God never turned His back upon a sinner. Man has turned his back upon God. Man has set his face toward the far country. It is for him to turn his face toward God. It is *man* who needs reconciliation to *God*. By saying this I am not lowering the standard of Divine holiness. In this use of the word reconciliation the New Testament standard of Divine holiness is never lowered. Man cannot be reconciled to God in his sin. What is needed is not God's reconciliation to man, but man's reconciliation to God, and that is impossible while he is still living in sin.

This attitude of welcome and love is not

the attitude man has any right to expect. If I have turned my back upon my Father's home, and have broken His heart, and destroyed His substance, and wronged His name, what right have I to expect that His face will still be toward me? I have a right to expect quite another attitude. We all talk much about our rights. Do we understand that our only right is that of eternal banishment from God's presence? We have none other, not only because we are of sinful nature, but because we are sinful actually. The right of every self-centred soul who has sinned against heaven is banishment from God. Yet God's mightiest work, His greatest concern, is that men should be reconciled to Him.

The reconciliation of God was the result of His own action as revealed in Christ, and needed no persuasion. The reconciliation of man must be by persuasion. Yet there can be no reconciliation of holiness to guilt, to sin, to wrong, save by the way of the Cross, save by the way of that for which the Cross stands, and which the Cross reveals.

How is it that God never turned His back upon man? With His holiness insulted, His righteousness denied, with that law upon which the safety of the universe depends violated, why did He not abandon man? The deepest answer to that question is to be found in the briefest statement, "God is love." Yet if I said no more than that I should do violence to the whole of Scripture revelation. Love cannot deny light. Light is an integral part of love. We have never understood the truth about God when we separate between His light and His love, between His righteousness and His mercy. God is the stern and unbending foe of sin because He is love. If you can persuade me to believe that God will excuse sin in any life, or under any circumstances, in that moment you persuade me that God is not love. It is the passion of His heart, the deep love of His nature which makes Him the sworn enemy of sin, and will never allow Him to sign a truce with it in individual life, in society, in the nation, in the world, or in the universe.

Theologians have often told us that love

is one of the attributes of God. Love is the sum total of the attributes. Love is to the attributes of God what character is to the characteristics of a man. Break up character, and you may speak of characistics. Break up the essence of God, and you may speak of attributes. Gather the whole of the characteristics, and know them in their true relationships, and you know character. Gather the attributes together, and the sum total is love. It is because of love that God never turned His back upon man; but that love is the sternest foe of sin.

Love is nevertheless mightier than sin. It suffers, and upon the basis of that suffering, is able to forgive, and in no other way. Love gathered into its own consciousness all the issue and outcome of man's rebellion, and the only thing which love can never forgive by the way of its suffering is refusal to be forgiven by love through suffering. The only sin which is unpardonable is the sin of rejecting the testimony of love in Jesus by the Holy Spirit. If I will not receive forgiveness based upon righteousness, which is the outcome of the suffering of love, the very love and suffering of God Himself, then God Himself, for love of His universe, cannot receive me into fellowship with Himself. These are the essential facts. It is by the way of Calvary that we have learnt these truths. In the mystery of the dying of this Person, the Lord Jesus Christ, there was wrought out into visibility that infinite and eternal truth. Do not imagine for one single moment that by the dying of the Man Jesus of Nazareth, apart from the fact that He was other than Man, the race has been redeemed. Do not for a single moment imagine that by the dying of a man upon the Cross, God was persuaded to change His attitude toward man. That which we see in the Cross did not begin at the point of the material Cross. The Lamb was slain from the foundation of the world. In the moment in which man sinned against God, God gathered into His own heart of love the issue of that sin, and it is not by the death of a Man, but by the mystery of the passion of God, that He is able to keep His face turned in love toward wandering men, and welcome them as they turn back to Him. Had there been no passion in His heart, no love, no suffering of Deity, no man could ever have returned to Him. Had He been none other than holy and righteous, and had there been no emotion, no tenderness, then He might have vindicated His holiness by the annihilation of the race. To know what God is we listen to some of the verses of the Old Testament. Go back to the beginning of beginnings and hear the voice in the dark, "Adam, where art thou?" My beloved and revered friend, Dr. Henry Weston, said: "That is not the call of a policeman; it is the wail of a Father over a lost child." Hosea, out of his own heart's sorrow, expressed the feeling of God's heart concerning the wandering, "How shall I give thee up, Ephraim?" That is God's attitude toward all sinning men. He has gathered up into His own Being, not by mechanical effort, but by the very necessity of His nature, all the suffering which issues from sin.

Men did not know it, and could not understand it; and therefore God came into human form and human life, to the actual-ity of human suffering, on the green hill and upon the rugged Cross, working out into visibility all the underlying, eternal truth of the passion of His love, that men seeing it, might understand it, and put their trust in Him. Therefore by this actual historic and material death, the reconciliation of man is alone possible.

"You .... hath He"—the Image of God, the Creator of worlds, the Head of His Church—"reconciled in the body of His flesh through death." Not that He conciled God to man, for he was God Himself; but that He through that death has made possible the reception to Himself of sinning men, and that through that death He makes His great appeal to man in his rebellion, calling him to turn back to God.

What is the need of man to-day? Why are men afraid of God? Those of you who are His own children fear the Lord and cling to Him. The man who does not know God is afraid that God will hurt him. Those who know Him are afraid lest they should hurt God. The difference is radical. One is slavish; the other is filial.

One drives us away from Him; the other keeps us close to Him.

Why is the man who slavishly fears God afraid? I will tell you. Go back to the early Genesis story. At the end of the day the man is hiding. Why did he hide? Had God changed? No. Man hid because he had changed—he had sinned. That is why men are afraid of God. It is because of their sin. They are afraid of God, and the fear keeps them at a distance from Him, and the fear is born first of all of actual sin, and then of consciousness of paralysis and inability to please Him.

God answers that fear in the Cross. He declares by that Cross that sin is borne, carried, put away. He affirms by that Cross that, though men are afraid of Him, He loves them with such love as never can be expressed or measured in human words. He announces by that Cross, that at infinite cost, by the mystery of the passion which knows no human measurement, He gives pardon and new life.

Then there is nothing for me to do other than to look into the face of Jesus, Who is Lord, and say, "He loved me, and gave Himself for me."

Theory of Atonement? Nay, verily, but the great *fact* of Atonement. Explanation of the Cross? Nay, verily, but the great healing *love* that wins through suffering; and will receive us just as we are, if we will turn our eyes from man to Him; and will blot out all our sin, and make us all He would have us to be.

THE CROSS AND THE SINNER

IV

THE CROSS AND THE SINNER

"In whom we have our redemption through His blood, the forgiveness of our trespasses, according to the riches of His grace."—EPHESIANS i. 7.

THE sense of God as personal involves conviction of His supremacy. It has been objected that personality ought not to be predicated of God, because personality implies limitation; but that is to misinterpret personality. It is of man that personality cannot be perfectly predicated, because man is limited. Perfect personality is unlimited. God alone is perfect in personality.

The sense of the supremacy of God creates the consciousness of sin. If our doctrine of God lose the note that affirms His personality, our doctrine of sin will lose the note that brings conviction. If God be known as personal and sovereign, man is conscious of sin. We may call it by any name we please—I care nothing for the name; we may speak of it as failure, as missing the mark, as coming short; the fact remains that directly man is conscious of God, and of His supremacy in the universe, he is also conscious of the fact that he has come short of the Divine requirement. That is conviction of sin. I am not now accounting for this widespread conviction, but I affirm that it is present.

I go one step further. The sense of God as personal perpetually causes a desire to be free from sin; or, in other words, a desire for forgiveness. These three things are interdependent. To destroy in either order is to destroy wholly. Deny the doctrine of the personality of God, and you immediately weaken the consciousness of sin, and consequently man becomes careless about forgiveness. Let a man become careless concerning forgiveness of sin, it is because his conception of sin is not that of disobedience, and such weakening invariably issues from some conception of God that dethrones Him from the place of actual supremacy in the universe.

THE CROSS AND THE SINNER 67

The message of the Christian evangel is to the sinner—that is, to the man who is conscious of God, and of his own failure; and who, in the deepest of his heart, would fain be free from failure. The message of the Cross is to that man. While the ultimate meaning of the Christian message goes out into that sinless life which lies beyond the present one, it begins with the forgiveness of sins. The first thing that Christ says to the soul who turns to Him is, "Thy sins are forgiven." That is not final; it is elementary. But it is fundamental.

In this text we discover: first, this first issue of redemption, "forgiveness"; in the second place, the method of redemption, "through His blood"; and finally, the source of redemption, "the riches of His grace." The Apostle moves back from the initial experience, and indicates the channel through which it comes, until finally, in one phrase full of beauty, he reminds us of the source from which the stream flows forth.

"The forgiveness of our trespasses"; that is the first issue of redemption.

68 THE CROSS AND THE SINNER

"Through His blood"; that is the method of redemption. "The riches of His grace"; that is the fountain head of redemption, the spring amid the eternal hills whence the great river flows. Or to state these things in the other order. The fountain head: "the riches of His grace." The channel through which the river flows: "through His blood." The gift the river brings: "the forgiveness of our trespasses."

I

First, then, "the forgiveness of our trespasses." This is so universally understood as a need—observe carefully that I do not say the method is universally understood—this is so universally understood *as a need,* that I do not propose to dwell upon it, save to emphasize the strength of the thought as it is here stated.

Sir Oliver Lodge has declared that the intelligent man to-day does not think about sin. I believe the intelligent man does think about sin, because he has to face the fact of sin. He may call it by other names. He may invent scientific

THE CROSS AND THE SINNER 69

terminology to describe fact of which he is conscious; but the fact is there, and the intelligent man never shuts his eyes to facts—he faces them.

Because man is universally conscious of sin, he is also conscious of the need for forgiveness. He may not explain the *need* as I would. He may have lost his sense of relationship to the throne of the Eternal. He may speak of forces where I speak of God. But there is no man who knows his failure who does not, in the deepest of him, wish it had not been, wish it could be undone, regret the fact of it. The passion for perfection is one of the common inheritances of the human heart. No man is really, in his deepest life, content with imperfection. Every man admires perfection. Every man would if he could realize it in every department of life. There is no man who loves sin. He may love the things that sin suggests to him, but every man is against his own sin.

In this text the Apostles makes use of two words, which we must note—"trespasses," and "forgiveness." The etymology of the Greek word here translated "trespasses" suggests a falling out—a falling out of line. Trench says that the word means falling, where one ought to have stood upright, whether wilfully or not. It is the fact of falling. This word you will find, as you study the New Testament, is used sometimes of what we in these days call the smaller sins, or faults; but it is also used of the final and most awful sin of actual and absolute apostasy. It is an inclusive term. It is a word which includes all those deviations from the will of God which trouble the soul of man. Swiftly and silently think back over the line of your own life. Trespasses! There they lie, back through the years. If we could undo some of them! Peccadilloes, faults, deviations from the straight line of duty; tragedies, vulgarities are all there! The word sweeps over the whole of them. I am not discussing the mystery of original sin. The Apostle does not refer to it here, save as these are the fruit of the underlying principle, save as these are the apples of Sodom growing out of the root which in itself is poisoned.

The etymology of the Greek word trans-

THE CROSS AND THE SINNER 71

lated "forgiveness" suggests freedom. The root idea is that of being "sent out," "sent forth." This particular word is variously translated in the New Testament, "deliverance," "liberty," "remission," "forgiveness." Let the text be read with some of these words substituted, "In Whom we have our redemption through His blood, the deliverance of our sins," "the liberty of our sins," "the remission of our sins." It is a word which recognizes all the bondage into which our sins have brought us, of guilt, of pollution, of power; and declares that by this redemption we are set free therefrom. Not free merely from the penalty. I did not name the penalty—not that the penalty is not included—but I named the things, which being removed, the penalty is also removed. Penalty is a consequence. Forgiveness is liberty from the guilt of sin, liberty from the pollution of sin, liberty from the power of sin. Forgiveness means far more than saying: Never mind, I will pass it over, I will make no further reference to it. God never forgives that way. He never violates the cosmic order by lightly passing over the activity of disorder which wrecks and ruins human life and human history. New Testament forgiveness I can never extend to my own child. I cannot free my child from the guilt of wrong done. I cannot cleanse my child from the pollution which has gathered upon his mind as the result of wrong done. I cannot break the power of habit in my child through forgiveness. Consequently, whenever I try to illustrate Divine forgiveness by human I fail; for the symbol cannot perfectly convey the infinite meaning. Forgiveness is to be set loose from sins, their guilt gone, their pollution ceased, their power broken. That is what the world needs. This is what the Christian message declares, and what Jesus Christ offers to men first. It is the beginning, it is not the last thing; but, blessed be God, it is the first!

II

Now concerning the method: "In Whom we have our redemption through His blood." It is impossible to read the New Testament without noticing the constancy of this figure. All the writers and teachers make use of it in one way or another. "Purchased with His own blood," "Justified by His blood," "Having made peace through the blood of His Cross," "Redeemed, not with corruptible things, with silver or gold .... but with precious blood .... even the blood of Christ," "If we walk in the light, as He is in the light, we have fellowship one with another, and the blood of Jesus Christ, His Son, cleanseth us from all sin." These are but illustrations. Reverently we ask: What is the meaning of it?

There are those who have taken objection to it, and have attempted to express the truth in some other way. They ask for a new terminology. I never object to new terminology—indeed, I prefer new terminology for a new thing, to the old terminology robbed of its essential heart and life and meaning. I am told we need a new terminology, and that it will be safe for us to say, *"redemption through His life."*

Let us think of this. It is perhaps by consideration of the suggested phrase that we shall begin to see the meaning of the great and awful and appalling words, "redemption through His blood." Is it not true that blood is life? Perfectly true. Under the Mosaic economy the requirements in this respect were direct and stringent. Either in so many words, or in other words equivalent, the declaration is repeated, "The blood is the life." These things were written long before science had come to illuminate them. I need hardly stay to remind you that men have only known anything concerning the circulation of the blood for about two and a half centuries; yet that discovery, in all its wonderful unfolding and explanation, does but add infinite meaning to the old Mosaic word. Scientific men tell us that in blood there are certain vital facts: resistance, so that the blood in healthy life life, maintains its temperature as against heat and cold; organization, so that if you break in upon the flesh, and close it again, the organism will be renewed by the action of the blood; fluidity, so that the blood contains in fluid form that which tends to solidity; and finally, hear the mystery of

THE CROSS AND THE SINNER 75

it! death, the final proof of life. "The blood is the life."

Remember that the flesh in man is the outward symbol of the man himself. Remember that the essential in human life is the spirit. Yet the blood most perfectly sets forth the essential. "The blood is the the life." It is a purely physical declaration, yet an absolutely true one.

The Bible, however, does not teach that a man is saved by that principle, but by the *shedding* of blood. Salvation is not through life lived, but through life poured out. It is not by the life of Jesus that we are redeemed; but by His life given up in the pain and suffering of a shameful death, of which death there is no sufficient symbol or method of expression other than that of the shedding of blood. Redemption is provided, not by the richness of His life possessed, but by the suffering of His life poured out. As the blood in the physical life is the symbol of the spiritual, so in the actual outpouring of the blood of the Man of Nazareth there was symbolized that infinite mystery of essential Love bending to suffering and pain and death, gathering into itself that which is against itself in inherent principle, and suffering, in order that through that suffering there might be accomplished something which cannot be accomplished without it. It is through the *shedding* of blood that there is remission.

The moment we destroy this outward symbolism of words, we inevitably begin to contradict the infinite mystery which lies behind them, and which they do symbolize. The moment we begin to say there is no virtue in the actual blood, the physical blood of long ago, we are on the verge of denying the lonely, separate suffering of God in Christ, through which, and through which alone, it is possible for forgiveness, which is at once freedom from the guilt and pollution and power of sin, to be pronounced upon men. I lay this emphasis here because, as I have said, the question is often asked: Why may we not get rid of the phrasing, Cleansed by blood, and say, Cleansed by life? Because when we get rid of the phrasing we get rid of the truth. It is not by the life, but by the life laid down; not by the richness and beauty of the ideal, but by the mystery of its breaking and buffeting and suffering and death that it is possible for forgiveness to be pronounced.

Concentrating the thought for a moment upon the Man Jesus, knowing that He is but the window through which we look into the infinite and eternal mystery which lies behind, let us very carefully understand that not by the beauty of the human example can He forgive sins; not by all the rich glory of the wonderful life that holds us in its thrall and fascination can He pronounce absolution; but only as that life was bruised, a symbol of the very bruising of the Infinite, for "God was in Christ." There can be no divorce between God and Christ if we would understand the Cross.

III

We pass to the last of these thoughts, which takes us back to the original source —"the riches of His grace." Our freedom from sin is through "the riches of His grace." The death which makes possible our freedom from sin is through "the riches of His grace." What a revelation of God we have here! I pause for poverty of words and for lack of ability to lead you to these great heights. One can speak of the realm of conscious sin, for how have we known it! One can say something in the realm of suffering through which we have been pardoned, or may be pardoned, for we know the Cross! But when man tries to pass behind these matters and come into those far-reaching, infinite things, expressed in this word, "the riches of His grace," what can we say? We can only reach these heights by coming again through the Cross. In the Cross the nature of God is revealed in His attitude toward the sinner. It is that of grace; not something sickly and sentimental, but the great necessity of loving; Love in action—that is grace; or, if you will, Love itself, that which precedes action, the thought, the will, the purpose; and we see the heart and nature of God in this unveiling of His thought and purpose toward sinning man.

Grace in the heart of God was not created by the Passion. The Passion was created by the grace. The work of the Cross, this blood redemption; the redemption of which blood and blood-shedding are the only fit sign and symbol—this work of the Cross did not persuade God to graciousness. God's grace did compel this Passion of the Cross, and therein is a revelation of the nature of God.

Therein also is unveiled the will of God in the work He did for the sinner. When man has sinned and is guilty and polluted and paralyzed, in order to his saving, Love will go to the uttermost extreme. We never know all the beauty of the declarations concerning love on the human plane until we see them placed in the light of the heavenly revelation. "Love is strong as death," mightier than the grave. Love will break through every barrier. The will of God become revealed in the light of this great Cross.

But more. Not only the nature of God and the will of God are revealed, but also the power of God. All these things are in our word "grace." Grace is that which is born amid the eternal hills; but it is also the river which proceedeth from the throne of God and of the Lamb. Notice Paul's word, "the riches of His grace," the fullness of His grace. There is a measurement for His grace. Take another of Paul's phrases, "the riches of His glory." What gleams of it we have had in creation, in government, in prophetic song and vision, in the hope that is in our heart of the ultimate victories! "The riches of His glory" is the measurement of "the riches of His grace." As is His glory, so is His grace; so that this selfsame Apostle, writing to Titus, brings the two things into juxtaposition. *"The grace of God hath appeared,* bringing salvation to all men, instructing us, to the intent that, denying ungodliness and worldly lusts, we should live soberly and righteously and godly in this present world, looking for the blessed hope and *appearing of the glory* of our great God and Saviour Jesus Christ." In that great passage the thought of Paul was fixed upon the two advents of Jesus: the appearing of grace when He came, the appearing of glory when He comes; the appearing of grace in the loneliness of His first advent,

His ministry, His patience, and His dying; the appearing of glory in the splendour of His second advent, and the triumph of His administration. Can you measure this? When you can measure this you can measure that. When you can understand the meaning of the glory which at last shall triumph, in the hope of which we rejoice even in affliction and limitation, then you can understand the fullness of His grace.

A spurious, latter-day refinement, which objects to the mention of blood, is both sickly and sinful. A deeper sentiment would be conscious that the awful bloodshedding of the Son of God is the most terrible revelation of the meaning of sin, and is in itself proof of the dire necessity for such means of salvation. Do not let us forget this. I want to utter this with all the solemnity of conviction. I pity from my heart the man who tells me he objects to the phrasing concerning blood. I pity him, for he is suffering from a soft, sentimental ignorance of his own heart, and ignorance of the actual deceitfulness and heinousness of sin.

They say that the Cross of Jesus is

vulgar! I know it. Never was there anything so vulgar in human history as the Cross of Jesus! But where is the vulgarity? It is in the sin that mauled Him and put Him there. It is your vulgarity. It is my vulgarity. It is the vulgarity that lies and cheats, that is impure, that laughs at sin, or speaks of it as though it were something to be pitied. It is the vulgarity that has lost its sense of the high throne of God and the white purity of His heaven. It is the vulgarity of the age which drags God off His throne and makes Him merely a force in His creation, and denies righteousness and purity. That is the vulgarity that lifted the Cross! Sin is so vulgar that it can only be dealt with by that which violates the essential life of God. The Cross? Yea, verily; but the rough, brutal Roman gibbet was only the expression in time of something far more terrible. Those two pieces of timber and a dying Man! Awful, terrible; but infinitely worse was the pain of God, which was invisible save through that Cross. In His rich grace He took hold upon sin and expressed, in the suffering of His only Son, its vulgarity.

Thank God, He did more, for that very Cross of blood and shame is radiant with the glorious light of the infinite Grace; for, even at the cost of such suffering as makes poor half-cultured man shudder, Love, determined on man's salvation, accomplished it. Yes, disease is vulgar; but the mother and the nurse who touch it, to heal it, are not vulgar. Contact with it in order to heal it is not vulgar. I come to the Cross to bow my head in shame, and smite my breast with remorse. Vulgar Cross; but that in it which is vulgar is my sin. Shining through it is the light that comes from the throne; and flowing through it is the great river of His grace.

Now hear me in this final word. You tell me that the only atonement possible to me is by my own suffering upward to something higher. If you could persuade me that God could be satisfied with such salvation, I cannot be satisfied with it.

"Out, damned spot!" That is the true cry of human nature. The stain cannot be removed without blood, and that which is infinitely more, and deeper, and profounder, and more terrible than blood, of which blood is but the symbol—the suffering of Deity.

Blessed be God, this is the evangel for me. Oh soul of mine, guilty, polluted, paralyzed, we have "our redemption through His blood, the forgiveness of our trespasses." There my conscience finds rest. There I begin a new life, lifting my eyes toward the ultimate ages, God's last purpose for me made possible because He is able to forgive my sins.

THE CROSS AND THE SAINT

V

THE CROSS AND THE SAINT

"'Becoming conformed unto His death.''
PHIL. iii. 10.

THIS brief passage of Scripture occurs in the midst of a wonderful piece of spiritual autobiography, in which Paul revealed the bearing of past experiences and of future expectations upon his then present life.

In the first part of the passage we are presented with a picture of the days before Christ apprehended him, as the Apostle declared to the Philippian Christians that, if there were any man who considered he had the right to boast in the flesh, he, Paul, had a greater right.

He next referred to a moment in his life when his whole outlook was changed, when his conceptions of things were radically revolutionized, so that he was able to write, "What things were gain to me these have I counted loss." It was a moment when he gathered up all the things which hitherto had been most precious to him, and casting them beneath his feet, trampled on them as worthless. It was a moment of which worldly men would speak as the occasion of a great renunciation, or of a great foolhardiness. In that hour he had turned his back upon his ambitions and upon all the things he had valued most; and they were not mean things, they were not base things, they were not ignoble things; they were the things of nationality, of blood, of morality, and of religion. Nevertheless, the vision he saw was of such nature as to make these most sacred things of his life appear in his eyes as refuse.

He then declared, that from the moment when Christ apprehended him, his one ambition, an ambition which had become an all-consuming passion, and constituted the driving force of his life, was that he might apprehend Christ.

That ambition he described in brief but suggestive words, "That I may know Him, and the power of His Resurrection, and the fellowship of His sufferings, *becoming conformed unto His death."*

These last words do not describe the consummation of his ambition; they rather reveal his conviction as to the only condition upon which that ambition could be realized.

"Being conformed unto His death" is not the ultimate experience; it is the initial condition. The Apostle did not mean to say; I desire to know Him, and the power of His Resurrection, and the fellowship of His sufferings, and then finally; I desire to be conformed unto His death. He intended rather to say: I desire "to know Him, and the power of His Resurrection, and the fellowship of His sufferings," *by* "becoming conformed unto His death."

All those who have been apprehended of Christ, who have seen the vision, and heard the voice, and known experimentally His victory over them, share the Apostle's desire to know Him, to know the power of His Resurrection, to know the fellowship of His sufferings. This desire can only be fulfilled as they become "conformed unto His death." Every living experience of

Christianity begins at the Cross. The experience of the Cross is not final, but it is fundamental.

We are not dealing in our present consideration with that value of the Cross with which our last subject had to do. Therein we considered the fact that the Cross is the manifestation of an activity of God in Christ, in which activity man in his sinful nature can have no part, but out of which activity a value is provided, which man must receive as the free gift of infinite grace.

We are now attempting to deal rather with the subject of that identification with Christ in His Cross, without which there can neither be true knowledge of Himself, nor experience of the power of His Resurrection, and of the fellowship of His sufferings.

This distinction can hardy be over-emphasized. The relation of the Christian to the Cross by faith is twofold; it is first that from which he escapes by Christ's presence there; it is then that into indentification with which he must come, if he

THE CROSS AND THE SAINT 91

would find his way into realization of the Resurrection life which lies beyond.

Our first relation to the Cross is that of the sense that in it, God in Christ experienced that from which we escape.

> I see the crowd in Pilate's hall,
>   I mark their wrathful mien.
> Their shouts of "Crucify" appal,
>   With blasphemy between.
> But of that shouting multitude
>   I know that I am one.

In this first approach to the Cross, man finds his place not on the Cross, but in the company of those who have put Christ there. Each one standing before it has to confess: It is my sin that binds Him to the tree, and not the nails which have been driven through His hands and His feet. He is there in my place. The height, the depth, the length, the breadth of it we cannot measure. The infinite mystery of it we can never fathom, for at the centre is God. We can no more lay our measurement upon the mystery of that atoning death than we can compress Deity into the compass of our finite understanding. In this sense we approach the Cross empty-handed, to receive the great and inestimable gift of grace "without money and without price."

That gift being received, by our acceptance of it we become identified with the underlying principles which have their supreme manifestation in the Cross. It is ours therefore, reverently to inquire what those underlying principles are, in order that we may understand what the Apostle meant when he spoke of becoming "conformed unto His death," or in the Galatian letter, of being "crucified with Christ."

I

First, then, the Cross was *the supreme demonstration of Christ's absolute conformity to the will of God.* That principle might be expressed in other terms. We might speak of His submission to the will of God, of His abandonment to the will of God, of His acquiescence in the will of God. Nevertheless, even though it may appear as though I were making a distinction without a difference, to my own mind there are suggestions in all these words of the

THE CROSS AND THE SAINT 93

possibility of elements which were not present. Submission may presuppose a previous rebellion. Abandonment and acquiescence are words which may leave upon the mind the impression that there had been some difficulty which was overcome by voluntary surrender. The word "conformity" does not include any such ideas.

The will of God has been the masterpassion of the life of Jesus. That may be granted without argument. It is clearly evident that in the mind of Christ there was the ever-present consciousness that the will of God was ultimately that of suffering and sorrow through which it would be possible for Him—that is, God—to communicate His grace to men. Thrice voluntarily in the story of the life of Jesus, we discover Him choosing the will of God even while He knew that it included suffering, sorrow, and shame: at His baptism, when He consented to be numbered with the transgressors; on the Transfiguration Mount, when He discussed with heavenly visitors the accomplishment of His exodus; on the occasion of the expressed desire of the Greeks to see Him, when, although His soul was troubled, He prayed, "Father glorify Thy name." He revealed the fact of His conformity to the will of God.

Thrice He overcame temptation in the power of His conformity; first, in the wilderness, when He declined to accept the suggestion that He should possess the kingdoms by a moment's homage to Satan; secondly when, in answer to the suggestion of Peter that He should spare Himself, He rebuked him in language full of unutterable sternness; and finally, in Gethsemane, in the mystery of that hour of agony, out of which He cried, "Father, if Thou be willing, remove this cup from Me"; and immediately added, "Nevertheless, not My will, but Thine be done." In the Cross we see the ultimate expression of this conformity, as our eyes rest upon a Man, not entering into conflict with God, but acting in conformity with His will.

Being "conformed unto His death," then, means that we begin our life where He finally expressed the master-passion of His own; and that as we receive the benefit of that Cross, coming to us as a gift of

THE CROSS AND THE SAINT 95

grace, by such reception we consent that henceforth our lives shall be mastered by the principle which He therein finally expressed. Becoming "conformed unto His death" means conformity to the will of God—that will, chosen as a principle, discovered in its plan, and obeyed in its programme.

It may be affirmed that this does not seem to be a difficult thing. It is perfectly true that it is not difficult when once the will has actually yielded; but it is in that act of yielding that the experience of the Cross is encountered. Conformity to the death of Christ does not consist in singing hymns about the will of God, or rejoicing in the intellectual apprehension of its perfection. It means rather the actual testing of every desire, and every affection thereby. All those which are out of harmony with that will must be destroyed. When the will of God is truly chosen as a principle, we no longer ask: What will our neighbours think? but, What will God think? no longer, What do we desire? but, What does God desire? no longer, What line of action will be pleasing to ourselves? but, What will please God?

Moreover, the principle must operate not merely in the great crises, but in the commonplaces of life. It is in these that we are made or marred. No man was ever ruined in a crisis, whose moral fibre had not already been weakened in the commonplaces. Reverently looking at the Cross again, recognizing it as the ultimate expression of the conformity of Jesus to the will of God, we remember the life which led to it, and recall some of its revealing declarations. *"I seek* .... the will of Him that sent Me"; *"My meat* is to do the will of Him that sent Me"; "I do always the things that are pleasing Him." Thus through all His life the mystic music of His declarations revealed the inner passion, the inspiration of His life; until at last, in continuity of co-operation with the will of God, He took His way to the Cross.

Becoming "conformed unto His death" means that we take up the Cross daily, and follow Him; that we consent to deny self and enthrone Him; that whether it be in the hour of some supreme choosing, or for the constant decisions of the passing moments; whether it be as to the calling which we are to follow, or as to the next thing we are to do; whether it be as to the choice of a life partnership, or as to the selection of the acquaintances of the passing days,—there is to be but one question asked: What is the will of God?

Those who have most fully entered into this experience will say that this is not death; and what they affirm is certainly true. Death is the way into life. That life is described in the previous language of the Apostle, "to know Him, and the power of His Resurrection, and the fellowship of His sufferings." That life however, is never entered but by becoming "conformed unto His death"; and in the moment in which we yield ourselves to the mastery of the will of God we inevitably pass through the experience of crucifixion.

II

In the second place, the Cross was *the place of Christ's utter outpouring of Himself in the service of men*. As we look again upon Christ crucified, three things are evidently set forth before our eyes: Christ's estimate of man's value; His answer to man's sin; and His method for man's saving.

No one who has truly seen the Cross of Christ can ever again speak of hopeless cases. He who declares that humanity is hopeless is looking at *it,* rather than at the Cross. Christ knew what we speak of as the hopelessness of humanity. He stood amidst the men of light and leading in His own day, and said, "If ye then, being evil, know how to give good gifts unto your children." "Being evil!" He was familiar with human philanthropy, and that goodness of heart of which to-day we hear much for did He not say, "Ye give good gifts unto your children"? but He also said, "Ye, being evil," and said it of men who manifested kindness of heart. When we know His estimate of evil, such language seems to be of the essence of pessimism. When we turn to the Cross we find that, while it still recognizes the fact of the evil of the human heart, it nevertheless reveals in unmistakable manner His estimate of humanity. Being evil, it is yet possible of redemption; it is worth dying for. He saw the stain, and understood its degradation and hopelessness as we cannot, save as we see it with His eyes. He was not deceived about human nature. "Being evil," nevertheless He died for men whom He thus described.

I repeat therefore, that no man who has looked into the love-lit eyes of the dying Christ can ever speak of another as hopeless. That is what His Cross meant. Tell me what you will about the pollution of the heart; I know it—I am human. Tell me what you will about the forces of evil that drive men astray from birth; I know them well, and no new-born philosophy can rid me of them. Yet over against all such declarations set this other fact; Christ considered that man, in the image of God, marred, bruised, broken, spoiled, was yet worth dying for.

"Becoming conformed unto His death" means that we take that estimate of humanity. If we come to the Cross with empty hands to receive the gifts of grace, and rejoicing in our gifts, neglect humanity, we are traitors, renegades, blasphemers; we crucify Christ afresh. If on the other hand, we come to the Cross of Christ with empty hands to receive the gifts of grace, and then hasten in the Passion of the Cross to break our bread to hungry men, to share our life with dying men, we are "becoming conformed unto His death."

"Becoming conformed unto His death" means also that we answer man's sin as He answered it, by pouring out our lives in sacrificial service, understandiing that we can only help in the saving of men by dying for them.

The lonely mystery of the pain of God is apart from us, but out of it flows the river, and of that river we drink and live. When we do so, we are committed to the principle from which the river flows, and henceforth we must have fellowship with His sufferings. When we accept His great salvation, we commit ourselves to fellowship, and thus enter into a contract of partnership. He poured out Himself for us, and "becoming conformed unto His

THE CROSS AND THE SAINT 101

death" means that henceforth we pour out our lives for others.

III

And finally, the Cross was *Christ's pathway toward His crowning*. He chose that pathway as against the suggestion of Satan, which was that of compromise; as against the suggestion of men, which was that of self-pity. He chose it because it was according to the purpose of God. He could have reached His throne in no other way. Through abandonment to the will of God and service of humanity, both at the utmost, the throne was reached. He might have made for Himself, as other men have done, a throne lasting a few years. He might, perchance, have created a dynasty continuing for centuries. But He could not have ascended the throne of empire, and held it through all ages, except by the way of His Cross. It was along the highway of His dying that He passed into the spaciousness of His reigning.

So also if we would reign in life we must be at the end of ourselves. We must give ourselves up for the sake of others. It is by the Cross that we triumph, not by policy, not by prudence, not even by passion, but by conformity to His death.

What throne do we covet? All the lesser thrones that are based on dust, I dismiss as unworthy of consideration. What place do we really desire of beneficent power, of helpful influence? Whatever it may be, there is but one way to find it, and that is by way of the Cross. We cannot reign in life until we have done with our own ambitions. It is always after some night of bruising and breaking that Jacob becomes Israel. Do not let us pity the man who limps, if his limping is the result of a night spent by the Jabbok. There is a limp which is a patent of nobility. In some lonely vigil of the night, when

> I lay in dust life's glory dead,

then

> From the ground there blossoms red,
> Life that shall endless be.

Thank God for those who are facing the great campaign, the flush of youth upon their cheek, the gleam and glow of health

THE CROSS AND THE SAINT 103

in their eye; spiritually ambitious, desiring to reign in life, as preachers, teachers, witnesses, as winners of souls; but let all such remember they must die in order to live, they must be conformed to His death in order to be transformed by His life from cumberers to conquerors.

Surely, if from that infinite unveiling of the Passion of God in the Cross, we are ready to take the gift of love, we ought to be prepared to answer the call of Christ which asks us, seeing that we have received the gift, to enter into fellowship with the Giver.

What is the hindrance? The question is asked, but none can answer it for another. The hindrance is often the fear of men, the fear of persecution, the dread of the world's misunderstanding. All such fear is evidence of lack of faith in the One Who calls us to fellowship with Him in the Cross. We are afraid of the sequence of abandonment to the will of God. We are like the men of Gadara. Jesus landed on their shore, and there found men devil-possessed; and found also an unholy traffic in swine. He flung the devils out of the men into the swine, and destroyed the traffic. The men of Gadara immediately said: Prevent His coming nearer. If upon the shore He rebukes us thus, and destroys our profits, what will He do if He be permitted to enter into our cities?

In answer to all difficulties, what shall we say? There is but one reply: Consider Him, behold Him, meditate upon Him, understand Him. He was rich. Can we measure that? Can we measure His riches? An Apostle spoke of "the unsearchable riches of Christ"! But, though He was rich, yet "for your sakes He became poor." Can we measure that? Can we measure His poverty? Consider Him. As we do so He says to us:

> "I gave My life for thee,
> What hast thou given for Me?"

Let us hold up the idol to which we cling in the light of His Cross. Let us bring that forbidden thing with which we should have parted long ago, into the presence of His Cross. Let us hold our fears face to face with His courage. Let us command

THE CROSS AND THE SAINT 105

our lack of faith to consider His ability to help and keep.

That is the final answer to all faltering in the presence of His Cross. If we can but see Him, we shall be willing to stretch out these hands that they may be nailed to His Cross. If we look at the Cross we cannot do it! If we look at our hands we dare not do it! But if we consider Him, we can, we dare, we do. "Becoming conformed unto His death." *His* death; it is the vision of the Christ that woos us to willingness to die.

"Becoming conformed unto His death." What then? We shall know Him, we shall know the power of His Resurrection, we shall have fellowship with His sufferings. Let the chapter be read again. Before we are through we shall discover the word "conformed" once more. But now the writing is not "conformed unto His death." It is "the body of our humiliation .... conformed to the body of His glory."

So, by identification with the Cross, the saint passes into identification with the glory which is to follow.

THE CROSS AND THE AGES
TO COME

VI

THE CROSS AND THE AGES TO COME

"Through Him to reconcile all things unto Himself, having made peace through the blood of His Cross; through Him, I say, whether things upon the earth, or things in the heavens."—COLOSSIANS, i. 20.

NO consideration of these words can be satisfactory which does not recognize that they are part of a greater whole. The Colossian letter was written with the express purpose of correcting prevailing error. It is both interesting and instructive to note in passing that the erroneous teachers are not named, neither is the heresy stated. Paul was too wise to give gratuitous advertisement to the teaching or the teachers.

If there are differences of opinion concerning the errors which he wished to correct, we are certainly in no doubt concerning the truth which he set forth. The subject of the Colossian letter is pre-eminently that of the glories of the Christ in His relation to His Church. Its supreme word concerning Christ is, "It was the good pleasure of the Father that in Him shall all the fulness dwell." The supreme word concerning the Church is, "In Him ye are made full." It is the letter of the *pleroma,* a word which cannot be translated without losing something in the process; although, if our word *fulness* be permitted its simplest and sublimest significance, it conveys the true idea.

The letter then, is the result of the conviction of the Apostle that a true understanding of the fact of the fulness of Christ, as it constitutes the fulness of the Church, will correct all false philosophies.

The passage, of which the words we are about to consider form a part, consists of one of the most remarkable declarations of the New Testament concerning the greatness of the Person of Christ, and the greatness of His work. These are both dealt with in their relation to God, to creation, and to the Church.

The greatness of His Person is set forth, first in His relation to God, in the words,

"The Image of the invisible God"; secondly, in His relation to creation, in the words, "The Firstborn of all creation.... In Him all things consist"; thirdly, in His relation to His Church, in the words, "He is the Head of the Body, the Church.... the Firstborn from the dead."

The teaching concerning the greatness of His work is inseparably connected with that concerning the greatness of His Person. In regard to His work as Revealer of God, "It was the good pleasure of the Father that in Him should all the fulness dwell." In regard to His work with relation to that creation of which He is at once the Source and Sustenance, His mission is expressed in the words, "To reconcile all things unto Himself." Finally, His work concerning the Church, of which He is the Head, is expressed in the declaration, "You, being in time past alienated and enemies in your mind in your evil works, yet now hath He reconciled."

Thus it will be seen that these two threefold statements answer each other. Let us make that still more evident by stating them as three twofold statements.

The greatness of Christ's Person in relation to God is that He is "the Image of the invisible God." The greatness of His work in relation to God is seen in the fact that "it was the good pleasure of the Father that in Him should all the fulness dwell."

The greatness of His Person in relation to creation is that He is "the Firstborn of all creation....and in Him all things consist." The greatness of His work in relation to that creation is expressed in the words, "To reconcile all things unto Himself....whether things upon the earth, or things in the heavens."

The greatness of His Person in relation to the Church is that "He is the Head of the Body, the Church." The greatness of His work in relation to the Church is that of the reconciliation of individuals, in order that they may be built into the Church.

The fulness of the Person creates the fulness of the work. The immeasurable glory of the Christ as He is, creates the immeasurable grace of the Christ as to what He is able to do in the centre, and to the ultimate circumfercence, of the universe of God.

The special message of the particular words selected for our present meditation is that God; through Christ the Image of God, the Firstborn of creation, the Head of the Church; by the blood of His Cross, does reconcile, not merely individual souls, but "all things....whether things upon the earth, or things in the heavens." I am perfectly conscious of the stupendousness of the theme. It is that of the ultimate meaning of the Cross. We shall endeavour to consider its teaching concerning the sphere of the reconciliation, the nature of the reconciliation, and the supply of the reconciliation.

I

The sphere of the reconciliation is declared in the words, "all things....things upon the earth, or things in the heavens."

When describing the glory of Christ in creation, the Apostle declared, "In Him were all things created, in the heavens and upon the earth," but when he speaks of reconciliation, he uses the opposite order, "things upon the earth....things in the heavens." The creative order was that of the heavens first, and then of the earth. The reconciling order is that of the earth first, and then of the heavens. It is not for us now to enter upon any discussion as to whether this planet of ours is indeed, as Dr. Wallace has suggested, the centre of the created universe. It is perfectly certain that there are far-stretching reaches of creation about which we know nothing. It is enough for us at the moment to recognize the fact that, for the purpose of our apprehension of the meaning of life, we are compelled to deal with the universe as circling about the earth on which we live. That may not be the ultimate truth. I do not know. Recognizing this necessity, the Apostle shows that the reconciliation begins here, and then affects all the heavens. That which demands reconciliation is here, but that which is here has exerted its influence to the uttermost bound of the creation of God.

This conception of the world at once lifts it, and our theme, into highest dignity and vastest importance. If we can but

THE AGES TO COME 115

grasp it, it will deliver us from all mean thinking about our own lives, about our own sin, and about our own redemption.

It is evident that the apostolic phrase, "things upon the earth," does not include man. He is first, and to him the Apostle returns presently. The phrase, as used in this statement, is equivalent to that of Jesus in His commission, "the whole creation," a phrase which this same writer made use of in his letter to the Romans. The sphere of reconciliation then is first that of the "things upon the earth."

That is not however the phrase which arrests and almost startles us so much as the one which follows it, "things in the heavens." This all-inclusive and comprehensive term has reference first to angels, those unfallen intelligences described elsewhere as "thrones, dominions, principalities, powers." These are all in some way included in the reconciliation which Christ wrought by His Cross.

This conception is a most remarkable recognition of the cosmic unity of the universe. Man is seen at the centre. Below him are all created things—things of the earth. Beyond him are the far-reaching realms which he is utterly incapable of perfectly understanding during the period of his earth-life. At the centre of everything Paul sees the Cross, and declares that by that Cross God reconciles all things unto Himself.

And yet the phrase, "things in the heavens," takes us one awful step further. The sphere of reconciliation is not only man, not merely the things of the earth beneath him, not alone the created things of the heavens above him; it is that of the very Being of God. Let us remember the words of the Psalmist:

<blockquote>Mercy and truth are met together;
Righteousness and peace have kissed each other.</blockquote>

Omitting for a single moment the declaration that these have met and kissed, let them be considered in separation. They all exist in the nature of God; mercy and truth, righteousness and peace. If we may reverently think of God as apart from the mystery of evil, we at once recognize the perfect harmony of these things. Mercy, which does not mean the pity that excuses, but the tenderness that bends over in love;

truth, which is integrity and uprightness, that which is stable and builds; righteousness, which is a straight line without deviation; peace, which is absolute safety,—all these co-exist in the nature of God.

The introduction into the universe of the principle of sin necessarily breaks up the harmony of these, and there is created the necessity for reconciliation within the very Being of God. God is a God of truth. In His universe a being violates truth. How is it possible for Him to bend in tenderness and love over such a one, whose action threatens the stability of the universe? God is the God of righteousness— that is, of that which cannot deviate from absolute rectitude. The introduction into the presence of essential Righteousness of that which contradicts it must make peace impossible. It is not by the caprice of a God Who is a despot, but because of the necessity of the essential facts of His Being, that the moment sin existed in the universe there was need for reconciliation, if mercy and truth are to meet together, or righteousness and peace are to kiss each other.

II

This consideration of the suggested sphere of reconciliation leads us immediately to our second line of consideration—that, namely, of *the nature of reconciliation,* which is expressed in the words, "unto Himself," or more literally, "with reference to Himself." Here again we begin on the lowest level, "things upon the earth."

What is the nature of the reconciliation which is necessary to the restoration of order? Fallen man misrepresents God, and so misgoverns nature. The result is chaos instead of cosmos, disorder instead of order. The only reconciliation which is worth while is the vanishing of chaos and the establishing of cosmos, the setting up of order in the place of disorder; or, in the words of the great prayer which Jesus taught His disciples, the supreme necessity is that His name should be hallowed, His kingdom should come, His will should be done on earth as in heaven. The reconciliation of things on earth is that of their restoration to the government of God, and the consequent restoration of a

THE AGES TO COME 119

perfect order throughout the world, of man, and of all beneath him in the scale of being; the healing of the wound, the closing of the breach, the gathering together into one of all things that have been scattered.

What then is the reconciliation that is necessary in the heavens? Peter declared in his letter that "angels desire to look into" the things of the sufferings of Christ and the glory that should follow. "Look into" is the translation of a strong word which means to peer into, to examine carefully. Bending over the world, the angels saw sin and suffering culminating in the experience of Christ. We must ever think of the angels as finite, of all these unseen principalities and powers as limited. We must remember that while loyal to the government of God, and serving Him with perfect satisfaction, they nevertheless watch the processes without perfect foreknowledge of the issues. It is impossible to remember this without recognizing the fact that their looking into these things is of the nature of inquiry. I am not suggesting that there was even incipient rebellion in the high places. There was surely an expectation that there would be some explanation of the mystery of that which they necessarily recognized as a rupture in the nature of God, resulting from the presence of sin in the universe. Angels needed an answer to such inquiry.

Again reverently we take a further step. Reconciliation, in order to completeness, must be such that in the Being of God there shall be possible the continued activity of mercy and truth, of righteousness and peace, so that violence is done to neither.

III

All this leads us finally to the consideration of *the supply of the reconciliation* which is revealed in the words, "Peace through the blood of His Cross." The Gnostic teachers were suggesting the necessity for the intermediation of angels. They were declaring the need for ascetic practices, urging voluntary humility and even the worship of angels. Paul, recognizing the necessity for reconciliation, not merely as between man and God, but throughout the universe, in the heavens as well as the earth, declares that it is provided in the "blood of His Cross."

In this connection it is necessary to repeat a warning and utter a solemn protest against the idea that when we speak of the Cross we refer only to a Roman gibbet, and to the death of a Man thereon. If He of the Cross were Man only, then all this writing of the Apostle is not only foolish, but vile dreaming, mirage, and nightmare, a delusion and a snare. On the other hand, if He of the Cross be the Image of the Invisible God, the original Creator and Sustainer, the Firstborn out of the mystery of death into life, then in the presence of His Cross I begin to tremble, and yet to believe the declaration that through that Cross He reconciles all things unto Himself upon the earth and in the heavens.

Through that Cross there is first the reconciliation of things upon the earth. This is established first by the creation of peace with God in the case of man, and then in the peace of God throughout the order over which redeemed man reigns. The process is a slow one as mortals count time. The travail is an agony, the conflict is unto death, but the victory is assured; and that victory is the reconciliation of all things upon the earth, first of man to God, and then of the whole creation to man in that peace of God which issues from the establishment of His throne, and the right relation thereto of all the kingdom.

Through that Cross also there is the reconciliation of things in the heavens. We call to mind again the picture of angels desiring to look into these things. As they did so, they became conscious of the profoundest depth of the mystery in the hour when Jesus died. It was the mystery of which we spoke in our first study, that of the death of a pure and sinless, and therefore, deathless Being. Personally, I can have no doubt about the literal accuracy of the Bible story that in the hour of that death the sun was darkened. My wonder sometimes is that it ever shone again. The angels saw in the mystery a revelation. They knew the Person Whom they saw die, and recognized that the death of the Christ must have some profound significance in the economy of God. Through

THE AGES TO COME 123

the death of the Lord they beheld man reconciled to God. They saw the salvation provided for the sinner in his loosing from his sins. They saw the resultant co-operation of the saints as, conformed to His dying, they came to living knowledge of Himself, shared the power of His Resurrection, and entered into the fellowship of His sufferings. They saw these saints bearing through to lower reaches of God's creation the renewing forces which had remade their own lives.

What effect, think you, had that working out into visibility of the passion and power of the love of God upon the watching angels? It was for them a new unveiling of God. In that Cross they saw Him as they had never seen Him. The essential Light of Deity shone whiter, for holiness was vindicated as never before. The essential Love of Deity shone redder, for compassion was manifested more perfectly. The essential Life of Deity was realized more fully, for all its values were revealed more absolutely. I can imagine that, as the Lord Jesus Christ died, and all the issues of His dying were revealed to them, angels borrowed the song of the Psalmist, and chanted to the measure of their own perfect music:

> Mercy and truth are met together;
> Righteousness and peace have kissed each other.

Reverently we come to the last fact in our consideration of this supply of reconciliation. Over two hundred years ago John Leland, a Baptist minister of Massachusetts, preached a sermon which he entitled "The Jarrings of Heaven Reconciled by the Blood of the Cross," in which he attempted to set forth a picture of the high courts of heaven and of the conflict within the very nature of God as the result of the presence of sin in the universe. The sermon may accurately be described as highly imaginative, but that is not a condemnation. There are matters so high that we can never hope to reach them save by the exercise of imagination.

We speak of law and love, of truth and grace, of justice and mercy, and so long as sin does not exist, there is no controversy between any of these. If there be no sin, law and love are never out of harmony

THE AGES TO COME 125

with each other; truth and grace go ever hand in hand; justice and mercy sing a common anthem. If the law be broken, what is love to do? If truth be violated, how can grace operate? In the presence of crime, how can justice and mercy meet? This is the problem of problems. It is not a problem as between God and man. It is not a problem as between God and the angels. It is a problem between God and Himself. It is answered in the Cross. "God was in Christ," from eternity, in the days of human manifestation, and surely also in the hour of the Cross. Thus, by the way of all the suffering consequent upon the conflict within His own nature, He found the way of reconciliation. By suffering wrought out into human history, and in the sight of all the ages through the Cross, He demonstrated that love meets law as it suffers, and fulfils it; grace satisfies the demand of truth by meeting all the issues of its violating; and mercy can operate upon the basis of justice, not because God has smitten and afflicted other than Himself, but because, in a mystery which baffles and bruises the intellect as it attempts to encompass it, God has gathered the whole into His own heart, and suffered to reconcile all things unto Himself.

Thus, as Christ is the Centre, Source, and Goal of the universe, His Cross is the centre, source and goal of reconciliation. The Ephesian letter is the complement of the Colossian. In that the Apostle teaches that through the Church the wisdom of God is to be manifested to principalities and powers in the heavenly places. Christ and His ransomed people are to exercise a ministry beyond that of to-day, which is initial and preparatory, through all the coming ages. That ministry is to be that of an unveiling of the profoundest thing in the heart of God: the love which, operating through self abandonment and sacrifice, ransomed, redeemed, and remade lost humanity. The angels will hear the music of love as they have never heard it, as the ransomed sing, "the old, old story of Jesus and His love." Sons of the morning are they, unfallen intelligences, who have never known the misery of sin, or its pollution; but they must hush their high anthems while the ransomed sing:

THE AGES TO COME 127

He loved us, and gave Himself for us.

Thus for all the universe and for the ultimate ages ever proceeding in beauty from the Being of God, the Cross will abide the supreme revelation of God, through which all creation will come to an understanding of His holiness and His love, the deepest and truest things of His Being.

What a theme for imagination, which nevertheless, is utterly incapable of encompassing all the glorious truth. We dream of the birth of ceaseless ages, of new creations, springing like fresh mornings from His wisdom and His might; and as in unfailing procession they appear, Christ and His ransomed Church will sing to them the song of redemption, and while they know the might and majesty of God in the wonder of their life, they will only come to a true apprehension of His heart as we tell them that He loved us, and "loosed us from our sins by His blood."

> In the Cross of Christ I glory,
>   Towering o'er the wrecks of time;
> All the light of sacred story
>   Gathers round its head sublime.

If by that Cross all things in the heavens are to be reconciled, and infinite peace is to follow, I dare trust it, notwithstanding all my sin and all my weakness. By the way of that Cross I am reconciled to God, and through it I find rest, infinite, eternal, undying. At last my rest shall be rest with the whole creation, for the cosmic order will be restored through the mystery of God's suffering as revealed in the Cross.

www.ingramcontent.com/pod-product-compliance
Lightning Source LLC
Chambersburg PA
CBHW050834160426
43192CB00010B/2015